Brian Read was born in 1939 in Essex and raised in East and South-East London. With no formal educational qualifications, in 1954 he left Secondary Modern School and became a trainee millwright and then a trainee groundsman before joining the Merchant Navy in 1955 where he travelled widely. In 1961 he embarked on a fire service career, first with the Devon County Fire Service, then the City of Plymouth Fire Brigade, and finally the newly formed Devon Fire Brigade. Whilst on duty in 1983, in the rank of assistant divisional officer, he sustained an injury that in 1986 resulted in his medical discharge.

Since leaving the fire service he has been a freelance writer, mainly articles for periodicals. His first book, *History Beneath Our Feet*, published in 1988, proved successful and after extensive revision underwent re-publication in 1995. *Cockington Bygones Vol 1,* published in 1999, the first of four volumes of a definitive history of this part of Torbay, received much praise. He has two sons and lived in the Parish of Cockington for 24 years. His interests include metal detecting, the study of antiquities, archaeology, antiques, history, walking, reading, gardening and travel.

COCKINGTON BYGONES

Volume Two

Front cover. Cockington Church 1891
(note chimney from the Mallocks fireplace) (DM).

Frontispiece and endpiece. Two of Sir Edwin Lutyens proposed shop signs (HE).

Chapter heading logo. A c.15th - c.16th century tinned copper-alloy strap-end with the
sacred monogram IHS, Latin abbreviation for Iesus Hominium
Salvator (Jesus Saviour of Men) depicted in niello, found in
Ladypark (PR).

V

Dedication

To Daniel and Patrick, for the privilege of sharing their formative years among the delights of the Parish of Cockington.

COCKINGTON BYGONES

A History of the Manors of Cockington and Chelston
and the Parish of Cockington
by

Brian Read

illustrated by

Patrick Read

Volume Two
Cockington Church, Cockington Court, and Hostelries

Portcullis  Publishing

First published 2000 by
Portcullis Publishing,
Meadow View, Wagg Drove, Huish Episcopi, Langport,
Somerset, TA10 9ER.

ISBN 0 9532450 1 2

Designed by Abbott Copy Centre, South Australia, 5007.
Typesetting and printing by S.P. Press, Cheddar, Somerset.
Cover design by Philippa Foster 5 D Design Services.
Shields of arms on back of cover drawn by Patrick Read.

By the same author:
History Beneath Our Feet 1988. Merlin Books.
History Beneath Our Feet 1995. Anglia Publishing.
Cockington Bygones Vol 1 1999. Portcullis Publishing.

Notes on Illustrations

Institutions and private individuals kindly provided some illustrations, whilst others are adaptations from earlier publications or especially prepared by © Patrick Read or the author. Each has one or more of the undermentioned credits after its respective caption:

Torquay Museum (TNHS), Waycotts Estate Agents (W), Vicar of Cockington (VC), Hugh Watkin (HW), Mr & Mrs Cook (C), Ian Smith (IS), Tom Mills (TM), Don Mills (DM), Bert Taylor (BT), Jim Short (JS), Patrick Read (PR), the author (BR). Photographs and drawings of artefacts are not to scale. Pictures of Lutyens signs by courtesy of the *Herald Express,* Torquay.

Contents

Chapter One
Cockington Church

Chapter Two
Cockington Court

Chapter Three
Hostelries

Bibliography

Index

List of illustrations

Plate

50. Cockington Estate staff and tenants Christmas and farewell party at the Drum Inn 1946.

Drawing, map

Abbreviations

Old English - OE
Middle English - ME

Acknowledgments

I am indebted to James White, William Winget, Hugh Watkin, Arthur Ellis, Charles Worthy, Richard Worth, Beatrix Cresswell, Deryck Seymour, John Pike and Joan Lang; their inquisitiveness and prolific pens made the updating of this volume a far simpler task. However, as with vol 1, primary sources helped remove the cataract of time, thereby revealing fresh evidence of yesteryear.

The following institutions and individuals provided invaluable assistance, to whom I am grateful: the Royal Armouries H M Tower of London, Torbay Borough Council, Torquay Natural History Society, Torquay Library; the Vicar of Cockington, Rev Anthony Macey; Blanche Ellis, formerly of the Royal Armouries; Commander P Cardale, for permission to publish extracts from *Arthur Mudge's* [of Plympton] *Diary*; Don and Tom Mills, Frank Palk, Bill Allan, Bert Taylor and Vince Horsely. Special thanks go to my youngest son, Patrick, for artwork and additional photography (his archaeological illustrating skill revealed the hidden secrets of two important antiquities in Cockington Church), and finally to my partner Val, for the time-consuming task of proof-reading.

As with the poem Cockington, published in vol 1, the author chose to publish herein Florence Kestrel Pridham's equally delightful poem "Cockington" (Harmony). Again, discovering precisely when it was composed and obtaining the necessary permission proved unsuccessful - any breach of copyright is unintentional and is the sole responsibility of the author. Thank you Florence Kestrel Pridham.

Forward

Perhaps the day will come when our descendants will ponder how it ever came about that so much of our most beautiful English landscape could have been sacrificed on the altar of the 20th-century urban planning. Paintings, photographs and written descriptions of lost beauty will remain to nourish the nostalgia of those who long for the peace and tranquillity of places such as those written about with such loving detail in these four volumes.

In the last days of the 18th century the British fleet sailed into Torbay and the elegant terraces and crescents of Torquay were built for the officers and civilians serving the Royal Navy in its fight against Napoleon Bonaparte. Until that time the main naval bases in Devon had been Plymouth and earlier Dartmouth and Totnes, and the beautiful wooded hills and deep red earth of Torbay had remained almost unchanged for hundreds of years.

I have a particular interest in the village of Cockington as my ancestors were lords of the manor there from the end of the 14th century and I was brought there to be christened in the church in the thirties. Although Cockington Court and its park and church are only a few hundred yards from the seafront of a thriving seaside resort, now anyone who visits the village armed with these volumes will be carried back in their imagination to a wonderful and uniquely Devonian rusticity.

I was asked to be patron of the Torbay Civic Society some years ago, and the conservation of the area which is the subject of these books is high on our priorities for conservation. Our knowledge will be greatly increased by reading this history, and also the enjoyment of visitors, and this can only be good for Cockington and its chances of survival.

Lord Falkland

House of Lords, London

Introduction

This history is the result of five years research into primary and secondary sources and landscape interpretation. Largely completed by 1989, problems arose with publishing the work as a single book, therefore as a practical alternative, four smaller volumes evolved:

Volume One **Emergence, Chelston, Livermead, Stantor Barton, and Field- and Place-Names.**

Volume Two. **Cockington Church, Cockington Court, and Hostelries.**

Volume Three. **Green Lanes and Lost Trackways, Water Supplies, Mills, Cockington Wood, Cockington Park, the Rabbit Warren, Beekeeping, Devon Rosery and Fruit Farm Ltd, Cockington Woods Farm, and Cricket.**

Volume Four. **Other Notable Buildings in the Parish, Crime and Punishment, Parish Fire Brigades, Cockington at War, Treatment of the Poor, Cockington Isolation Hospital, and Schooling.**

Since the publication of vol 1 of this series, a lost *1801 Plan of the Parish of Cockington with part of the Parish of Marldon* (hereafter *1801 CEM*) has reappeared - secure in the Plymouth and West Devon Record Office. Among other things, this rediscovery (in reality a map of the land owned by Roger Mallock II) defines precisely which section of Stantor Barton land formed part of Cockington Estate at the commencement of the 19th century (whether the same Stantor Barton land as that purchased in 1654 by Roger Mallock I is uncertain). This means that the latter Eastleys and William Adams were probably tenants (see vol 1). Additionally, certain detail on the *Maps of the Eastern and Western parts of Cockington District*, both especially compiled for this history, in some instances is perhaps slightly inaccurate. Henceforth, however, where obvious anomalies occur, an informed opinion is provided.

Cockington's venerable church is already well recorded; herein is a revision of the more important details of its history, architecture and archaeology. Covered also are aspects omitted by earlier writers. The sequential approach adopted will allow the reader to perambulate the church and perceive most aspects dealt with here (notwithstanding, access to secured areas is only by permission of the vicar).

When considering Cockington Court's early history, one has a more difficult task when researching due to a paucity of primary archival material. Much of the architectural subject matter of this chapter remains visible (likewise, some parts of the Court are accessible only with permission from Torbay Council).

Concerning the sites of former hostelries (herein considered as either alehouses, taverns or inns) in the parish, primary and secondary archival sources provide a dearth of evidence; however, by combining history with landscape interpretation, one is able to arrive at a reasoned exposition. The history of the famous *Drum Inn* is somewhat easier to uncover, but, curiously, much has been bypassed by other writers. Unfolded here, for the first time in one document, is its fascinating story.

"Cockington"
(Harmony)

Blest Cockington our pure delight
A rural "Home" for Squire or
Knight.

Or lovely Dames of high degree
And folk of no great Ancestry
Let all in harmony can move
According to the "Law of Love".

Thy stately Court will e'er express
Majestic aim, Pride ne'er distress
The humble cottage thatched and
meek.
Where wholesome toil the labourers
seek
For all in harmony doth move
According to the "Law of Love".

That Rhododendrons grand and
gay
Methinks will ne'er presume to say
That periwinkles, pansies, stocks,
Forget-me-nots and hollyhocks
Are in that Universal plan
A very common gift to man.

Thine Ancient Church, serene, doth
hold
A place where man will e'er unfold
Gods law of perfect harmony
Of joy, peace, and humility
The "Law of Love" and unity
Above class strife and enmity.

Florence Kestrel Pridham

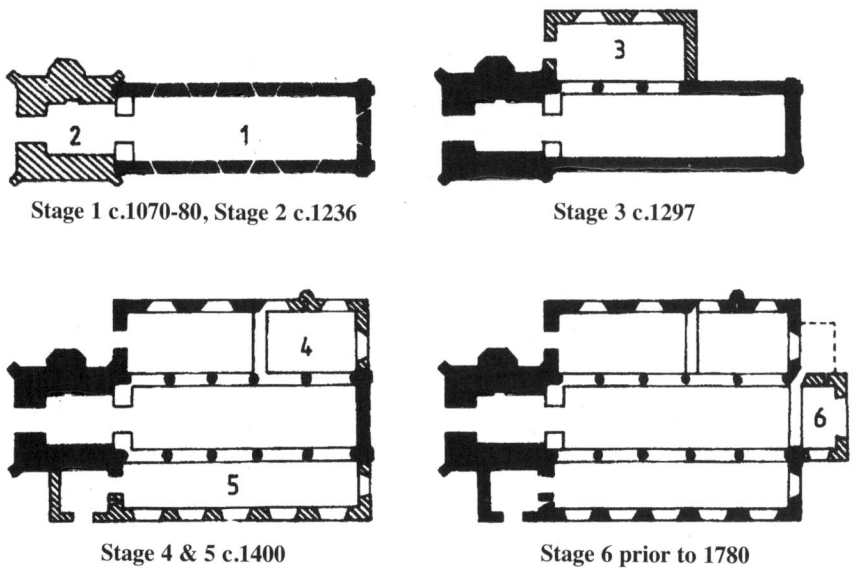

Stage 1 c.1070-80, Stage 2 c.1236   Stage 3 c.1297

Stage 4 & 5 c.1400   Stage 6 prior to 1780

Fig 1. Development stages of Cockington Church (open-work denotes demolished walls, hatching, new walls), redrawn from Hugh Watkins sketch (PR).

Chapter One

Cockington Church

Cockington parish forms part of the Deanery of Ipplepen, Archdeaconry of Totnes and Diocese of Exeter. Of all the parish buildings the typically Devonshire Perpendicular church of St George and St Mary (a Department of the Environment Group B church), which occupies an idyllic position south of Cockington Court, is the best chronicled, both by the written word and by illustration. Perhaps the most pleasing of these early pictures - a delightful c.1870 oil-painting by Edward Noke - hangs in Torre Abbey.

The presence of an Anglo-Saxon church on the site is unproven; nonetheless, William de Falesia possibly built a small chapel c.1070-80 for the use of his own family - if they ever lived at Cockington (see vol 1). Watkin surmised that the present church evolved in six main building stages: the original chapel covered the nowadays nave, c.1236 the tower, 1297 slightly more than the half of the north aisle, c.1400 the remainder of the north aisle and the west porch parvise, and prior to 1780 the chancel. Ellis explained that Churches with dual dedications are uncommon:

'St George of Cappadocia was always considered to be the patron saint of soldiers and that William de Falesia probably dedicated the church to his favourite saint. This probably remained the dedication until 1236 when the Canons of Torre gaining permission would have decided to add the dedication of St Mary'.

The French and Welsh connections

When Robert Fitz Martin bequeathed Cockington to his son Roger, Cockington Chapel and its two farthings of sanctuary land passed to the Abbey of St Mary and St Dogmael at Camois, Pembrokeshire, founded by Robert Fitz Martin c.1113-15. This Welsh abbey's mother abbey was at Tiron in the province of Main, France, and an entry dated c.1113 in its *Cartulary* provides the first documented evidence of Cockington Chapel.

The White Canons of Torre Abbey

William Brewer, lord of the manor of Tormohun, founded Torre Abbey in 1196 on the site of an Anglo-Saxon manor house built by Alric (presumably the same Alric mentioned in vol 1). The monks who came to the foundation were priests of the Premonstratension Order, known as Canons Regular of Prémontré, commonly called the White Canons due to their white cassocks worn in honour of the Virgin Mary.

It must have been extremely difficult for the Abbot of St Mary and St Dogmael to minister the needs of his distant chapel; for this reason, perhaps, in January 1203 he decided to rid himself of this nuisance by leasing Cockington Chapel to Torre Abbey for three marks (one mark equalled a weight of metal worth 128 silver pennies) down and a yearly rental of 5/-, where it remained for almost 679 years. On 18 July 1469 Torre Abbey acquired the chapel for £63.6s.8d. At that time Cockington was a chapel of ease of the Parish of Tormohun, of which St Saviour's was the parish church. St Saviour's assumed the care of Cockington Chapel, and for the whole of the monastic period the White Canons conducted services at both houses.

After the Dissolution

On 25 April 1539 Torre Abbey surrendered to Henry VIII. It is believed that sometime between the Reformation in the 16th century and 1628, Tormohun and Cockington separated. However, the little church at Cockington remained under St Saviour's wing, with its vicar having jurisdiction over both houses until the appointment of Cockington's very first vicar, Rev Thomas Sole Rundle, on 19 December 1881.

In the period 1882-3 the church underwent a partial restoration; Richard Mallock paid for work at the east end. Apart from extensive repairs, other work took place: the installation of carved bosses to relieve the chancel roof, walling-up the rood loft doorway, the north aisle's west doorway fitted with an oaken door, and finely carved stalls of oak placed in the chancel. The discovery in a blocked-off niche (the whereabouts of which is uncertain) of the Commonwealth Chalice (or Cockington Chalice) occurred during this refurbishment. Cockington Parochial Church Council loaned this oldest surviving piece of Cockington Church silver - crafted in c.1660 and stamped with the makers mark RL surmounting a fleur-de-lys - for display in Torre Abbey.

Plate 1. Commonwealth (or Cockington) Chalice, Torre Abbey 1989 (PR).

Sixteen twenty-eight is the first date recorded in the *Baptism Register*, and the *Marriage* and *Burial Registers* commenced in 1632. In 1884 Rev Rundle published the first issue of the parish magazine, and 1890 saw the appointment of a curate. For centuries, first candles and then smelly oil-lamps illuminated the church interior; electric lighting arrived in 1935.

Damage sustained during World War II revealed the ravages of Death Watch Beetle in the original Devon-type wagon-shaped roof; its replacement occurred between April 1949 and July 1950. Public donations accounted for roughly half the cost of £10,000 and the balance came from diocesan funds. The Lord Bishop of Exeter, Dr Robert Mortimer D D, dedicated the new roof on Saturday 16 September 1950; whilst at the church he dedicated two oaken panels presented by Mrs Gilham in memory of Arthur Frederick Gilham her late husband.

After a lapse of 449 years Rev Anthony Macey has resumed the medieval practice of celebrating mass every Wednesday, at 1030 in winter and noon in summer, marked with an especially composed prayer for William and Johanna de Cockington. This custom originated c.1330-45 when William de Cockington granted the White Canons of Torre Abbey the right to divert water from Sheryl Stream (alias Sherwill Water or Stream). In gratitude the canons interred William and Johanna in the Abbey church and granted them a chantry and a mass celebrated each Wednesday at Cockington Chapel, except Feast days when it was the day before or after.

Plate 2. The Vicar of Cockington, Rev Anthony Macey (right)
and Curate, Rev Timothy Pilkington outside the main west
door of Cockington Church 1988 (BR).

The Churchwardens' Accounts

Cockington's *Churchwardens' Accounts* (hereafter CWA) survive from only 1656, nonetheless they disclose much about parish life. From the numerous disbursements concerning the church, hereunder are but a few concerning 'vermin' control and repairs to the building:

'1733	For a Thousand of Shindles [shingles]	00.07.06.
1767	Pd for killing a bager	00.02.00.
1768	Paid for killing 4 Hedge hogs	00.01.04.
1769	Paid for killing a fox	00.03.04.
1773	Paid for 8 niches of reed for the church roof	01.08.00.
1780	Paid for four Nitches of reed, and hund spears	00.01.00.
1816	For 1 Nittch Reed	00.05.00.'

These entries imply shingles covered all or part of the church roof for much of the 18th century, whilst thatch prevailed at other times in the same century and the early 19th century.

The tower

The Romanesque tower, surmounted by a crenellated-parapet, one of few remaining such church towers in Devon, is 20m high; its west wall is c.2m thick and the east wall c.1.13m. Piercing the west wall of the tower is the main entrance to the church which is provided with a robust oaken door. Attendant with the door a stout oaken beam, c.1.91m long, which when drawn across the inside and secured in wall sockets, ensured the exclusion of undesirables.

Reputedly contemporary with the tower, a ground floor wooden door, which once had a similar lock as the main door, provides ingress through the north wall where well-worn stone stairs wind in an external turret to upper levels. A blocked-up opening in the lower half of the door formerly allowed any occupant of the tower to receive food and drink.

A doorway leads from the staircase into a possible former sanctuary or priest's chamber fitted with a fireplace and flue; nowadays it is the bell-ringing chamber. The occupant perhaps stored victuals in a small niche in the wall. Wooden boards on the south wall are thought to be remnants of the original High Altar reredos allegedly removed during the 1882-3 restoration; interestingly a letter from Mary Janet to her cousin Richard Mallock refutes this by implying the installation of the new reredos occurred in 1881. The bell-ringing chamber door and two others leading from the stairs to upper floors are perhaps also contemporary. On the south wall of the bell-ringing chamber is a memorial plaque:

TO THE GLORY OF GOD AND IN MEMORY OF
ALFRED JAMES WILLS
JOINED THE TOWER 1930 CAPTAIN 1945 TO 1954
RETIRED 1960
HILDA MABEL EVELYN HEAD
JOINED THE TOWER 1947 - VICE-CAPTAIN 1955 TO 1968
DONALD MARTYN STEPHENS
A MEMBER OF THE TOWER 1966 TO 1969
— — — — — — — — — — — — —

THIS PLAQUE WAS GIVEN BY THE WIDOW AND
FAMILY OF DONALD MARTYN STEPHENS
EASTER 1970
— — — — — —-LAUS DEO— — — — — —-

Plate 3. Main west door, Cockington Church 1989 (note medieval beam lock) (BR).

Plate 4. Door leading into the tower, Cockington Church 1989
(note blocked-up opening lower left) (BR).

Plate 5. Door leading from tower stairway into the bell-ringing chamber,
Cockington Church 1989 (BR).

The bells

Affixed under the tower is a brass plaque inscribed with details of Cockington's bells. In 1553 the Church Goods Commissioners found 'At Cokynton iii belles yn the towre their'. The CWA has many disbursements for the 'Tolling of ye Bells' at funerals. A 19th-century estimate reads 'Take the present three old bells and recast them to five, and hang them in the tower, for the sum of £160'. Structural defects discovered in the belfry delayed recasting, therefore in 1908, for £360, the chamber immediately below became the new belfry. Removal of the three badly cracked and unusable bells occurred in 1909; after recasting in the same year two were re-hung. The third bell, the Commonwealth Bell cast in 1653, did not warrant recasting, therefore in 1932 it found a new home in the north aisle where it still resides. The church acquired three new additional bells in 1909 and another in 1910, raising the number of bells to seven, of which six are functional.

Coins of Charles I provide novel punctuation in a reversed inscription around the circumference of the Commonwealth Bell: GREGORY [coin] ALWARD [coin] PETTER [coin] PERNELL [coin] :: R [coin] :: H :: [coin] WE. L. Rubbings revealed that only four coins are apparently extant, these being much abraded hammered silver halfcrowns. Gregory Alward and Petter Pernell were churchwardens: the initials are perhaps those of bell ringers.

Of the two bells recast in 1909 the tenor is inscribed A. H. 1620. RECAST MARCH, 1909, JAMES HENNING, VICAR, W. WILKINSON COX, J. A. MERCER, CHURCHWARDENS, and the treble RECAST MARCH 1909, THESE FOUR BELLS WERE DEDICATED LADY DAY 1909. Inscriptions on bell three and bell four read CHARLES H. MALLOCK, M. IRIS MALLOCK, COCKINGTON COURT. The fifth bell bears the inscription THE GIFT OF WILLIAM JOHN TANNER FOR REMEMBRANCE BEFORE GOD OF EMILY CLARA HIS WIFE. AT REST FEB. 10th 1908. DEDICATED SEPT 29th 1909. The Cary Bell's, the sixth and the smallest bell, inscription reads THE CHURCH OF ST. GEORGE AND ST. MARY, COCKINGTON, TO THE GLORY OF GOD AND IN MEMORY OF MANY CARY'S BURIED HERE. AD 1371-

1634. GIVEN BY COL. LUCIUS CARY AND LOUISA HIS WIFE, OF TORRE ABBEY. AD 1910.

In November 1911 Rev James Henning quoted in the parish magazine a poem written in 1870:

> ' "The Bells of Torquay"
> We are before all in time
> Says Torre's sweetest of chime.
> But we ring in more people
> Says Upton Church Steeple.
> I ring in more Dons
> Says the bell of S. John's.
> But what of your Divinity?
> Says the tinkle of Trinity.
> Come here my rebukes
> Says the bell of S. Luke's.
> I think I preach well
> Says the Ellacombe bell.
> I've the sweetest of quires
> Says the young S. Matthias.
> We are all left in the lurch
> Says Cockington Church.
> We have room to improve
> Say all bells as they move.'

Rev Henning suggested that the following addition would be fitting to make the poem complete:

> 'The Cockington bells, o'er hill and o'er dale
> Says S. George and S. Mary, our patrons, we hail.'

Plate 6. Fragment of reputed old reredos in the bell-ringing chamber, Cockington Church 1989 (BR).

Plate 7. The Commonwealth Bell, Cockington Church 1989 (BR).

Plate 8. Rev Henning, Vicar of Cockington 1895-1916 (C).

The tower clock

The tower's second chamber, between the belfry and the bell-ringing chamber, hides a marvellous old clock. An entry in the CWA reads '1724 New Clock this Year charged at …' (no disbursement). This entry, and others, tell of an older clock at Cockington Church:

'1684   Phillip Stuck have done work on the clock   00.04.00.
1684   Paid to George Kan for keeping the Clock   00.01.00.'

Archival evidence fails to explain the origin of this earlier clock - its attribution is perhaps the later Middle Ages or Tudor period. The CWA disclose a continuing story of maintenance, but, sadly, it seems the current clock has not worked within living memory.

Between 1728-47 Richard Ball was responsible for keeping the clock, receiving 10/- per annum for his labours. In 1745 his wife gave assistance 'For [?] Roping yea Clock', being paid 10/- for her trouble; she seems to have been the keeper in 1748 and 1749, respectively, receiving 10/- both times. Their daughter Charity undertook this duty betwixt 1750-2, collecting 10/- for each of the first two years and 7/6d the third. The sample of CWA disbursements continues:

'1727	Paid Candells & oyl for the bells & the Clock	00.01.06.
1731	The Clockmaker for mending the Clock	00.19.00.
1749	A boy and a horse to fetch Stones for the Clock	00.10.00.
1749	Edward Hydon for making wight Stones for the Clock	00.04.07.
1762	Paid Mr Pike for mending the Clock	10.10.06.
1777	Mr Hearder for Cleaning & regulateing the Clock	00.07.06.'

Hanging under the tower
On the north wall

The rowel-spur

The reopening of the parvise concealed squint on 23 October 1914 revealed an iron rowel-spur complete with two original spur-leathers (one broken). These artefacts probably became secreted herein during building alterations in 1720, but why and by whom is an enigma? A romantic story conceived c.1918 credits the spur to Sir Henry Cary - allegedly lost by him when seeking refuge from a Civil War skirmish. At this time even the lord of the manor observed the long-standing prohibition against the wearing of spurs in church, therefore it is possible that a surprise attack on Sir Henry whilst at prayer caused him to leave behind a spur as he attempted to flee.

An archaeological illustration, commissioned especially for this book, revealed a fer-de-moline, a millrind (the iron from the centre of a millstone) - a heraldic or pseudo-heraldic device - on each side of the spur. A foremost authority on spurs, Blanche Ellis, reported that to find a heraldic device on a post-medieval spur is extremely uncommon, which makes the Cockington piece a very interesting example indeed. No contemporary prominent Southern Devon family had such a device in its coat of arms, crest or livery badge, implying the motif is purely decorative. Blanche commented that the spur's attribution is probably c.1590 - c.1640 and the product of an English spurrier, made for wearing on the left foot and definitely a functional spur and not specifically for funerary purposes. The above evidence implies that this spur wasn't Sir Henry Cary's, but actually belonged to Sir George Cary and formed part of his funerary achievement.

Cockington Fire Brigade memorial

An inscription:

5 MEN OF THE COCKINGTON FIRE BRIGADE VOLUNTEERED FOR SERVICE IN THE SOUTH AFRICAN WAR. ONLY ONE, GEORGE S. SANDERS, DID NOT RETURN HOME AGAIN. DIED AT MAITLAND, CAPE COLONY 27/11/1900. BURIED AT WOODSTOCK CEMETERY, CAPE TOWN.

Beam fragment

During repairs executed in April 1965, workmen removed from the tower roof a fragment of oaken beam, carved with the date 1767 and initials WH. The person responsible for this piece of 18th-century graffiti is unknown; perhaps it is a craftsman's mark?

Plate 9. Cockington Church clock 1988 (BR).

Plate 10. Iron rowel-spur, Cockington Church 1989 (BR).

Plate 11. Inscription on fragment of oaken beam, Cockington Church 1989 (BR).

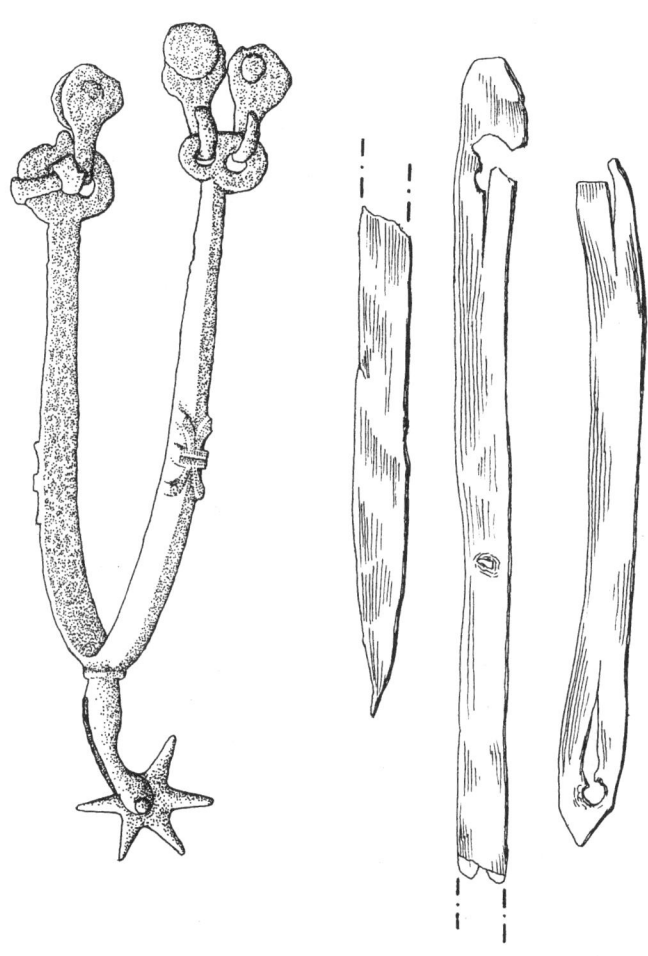

Fig 2. Iron rowel-spur, Cockington Church (note millrind) (PR).

The south wall

Affixed here are a cast-iron depiction of the Last Supper, a memorial inscription, and three faded charity boards dated 1702:

Plate 12. Cast-iron depiction of the Last Supper 1989 (BR).

1834
THIS WEST WINDOW
IS DEDICATED TO THE
MEMORY OF EMMA
HIS WIFE BY
GEORGE ARDEN MALLOCK

SIR GEORGE CARY KNIGHT BY DEED SETTLED ON TRUSTEES IN TRUST YE YEARLY RENT OF THIRTY POUNDS OUT OF THE MANORS OF COCKINGTON AND CHELSTON FOR EVER FOR YE REPAIRATION SEVEN ALMSHOUSES THERE BUILT AND FOR YE RELIEF OF THE POOR PEOPLE THEREIN FROM TIME TO TIME PLACED BY PAYMENT OF TWELVE PENCE A PIECE WEEKLY, AND AT CHRISTMAS YEARLY FOR EVER A NEW FRIZE GOWN AND A NEW SHIFT FOR EVERY SUCH POOR PERSON NOT EXCEEDING SEVEN PERSON AT ONE TIME TO BE CHOSEN OUT OF YE SAME PARISH BY YE OWNERS OF THE MANOR HOUSE, WITHIN 28 DAYS AFTER THE DEATH OF ANY SUCH PERSON, AND FOR DEFAULT OF SUCH CHOICE THEN THE SAME TO BE MADE BY THE BISHOP OF EXETER, AND THE SURPLUS OF THE £30 SHOULD BE EMPLOYED TO THE USE OF SUCH OF THE SAID POOR, AS SHOULD BE SICK AND FOR SUCH NECESSARY Dr RATIONS FOR THE BETTER RELIEF OF SUCH POOR PEOPLE.

MR THOMAS RIDGWAY GAVE FIVE POUNDS TO BE LENT OUT INTREST, WHICH INTREST WAS TO BE GIVEN TO THE POOREST PEOPLE OF THIS PARISH AT EASTER YEARLY FOR EVER.

Mr SOUTHCROFT WAYMOUTH GAVE TEN POUNDS TO BE LENT OUT AT INTREST, WHICH INTREST WAS TO BE GIVEN TO THE POOREST PEOPLE OF THIS PARISH AT EASTER YEARLY FOR EVER.

Mr ROBERT BALL GAVE FIVE POUNDS TO BE LENT OUT AT INTREST, WHICH INTREST WAS TO BE GIVEN TO THE POOREST PEOPLE OF THIS PARISH AT EASTER YEARLY FOR EVER. Mr JOHN WAYMOUTH NOW GIVES FIVE POUNDS TO BE LENT OUT AT INTREST, WHICH INTREST IS TO BE GIVEN TO THE POOREST PEOPLE OF THIS PARISH AT EASTER YEARLY FOR EVER.

The windows

During the 1882-3 restoration £96 was paid for new bell-chamber windows, and an unspecified amount spent on carefully preserving extant venerable painted-glass in the aisles. World War II bomb damage destroyed most of the original glass, however, salvaged fragments were re-fixed in new windows, the oldest being 13th century in the central window of the north aisle; these perhaps depict St Paul or St Martin of Tours. The same window holds a 15th-century letter M that probably refers to St Mary the Virgin and apparently has no connection with St Martin or the Fitz Martins. Surmounting the Romanesque arch over the west door in the north aisle - formerly the entrance to the de Cockington Chapel - are four painted-glass windows depicting a bishop, a canon, St George and St Mary; until 1892 they were obscured by the organ.

Plate 13. Painted-glass in the north aisle's central window, Cockington Church 1989 (BR).

Plate 14. Painted-glass windows over the west door of the north aisle,
Cockington Church 1989 (BR).

In memory of his wife Mary, who died on 1 June 1878, Richard
Mallock installed a stained-glass window of three lights above the altar in
St George's Chapel; each light depicts two scenes from the life of our
Lord. On 4 January 1950 the Bishop of Plymouth, Rt Rev Norman H
Clarke, unveiled and dedicated over the High Altar a new window
portraying Christ reigning in Glory with figures of the Virgin and Child, St
George and St Michael. The south wall of the chancel has a striking
stained-glass window beneath which is the inscription:

FOR REMEMBRANCE BEFORE GOD OF RICHARD MALLOCK
BELOVED.
AT REST JUNE 29. 1900.
THIS WINDOW IS DEDICATED TO HIS WIFE
ELIZABETH EMILY

The painted-glass in the second window from the west in the south aisle is perhaps 15th century and comprises 11 pieces depicting St John the Evangelist, St James of Compostella garbed as a pilgrim complete with staff and purse and a scallop-shell pilgrim's badge pinned to his hat, St Peter and St Andrew. This glass originally formed part of a large memorial window probably installed by, or in memory of, Robert Cary (insufficient clarity to photograph). Surmounting the tower main door is a window of clear glass installed by George Arden Mallock in memory of his wife Emma.

The nave
Robert Cary's font

At the western end of the nave, representing entry into the church, stands the octagonal font presented to the church in the 15th century by Robert Cary as a thanks-offering for having his land restored by Henry VII (see vol 1). Carved from Caen stone, it has a different coat of arms, each commemorating a family marriage, in each of its eight panels. In heraldry their description is thus:

1. (argent) on a (bend) sable three roses of the field Cary impaling three lions passant Carew. Robert Cary's first wife was Jane, daughter of Sir Nicholas Carew of Ottery Mohun.
2. Cary impaling three swords point downwards Pawlett. Elizabeth, daughter of Sir William Pawlett, mother of Robert Cary.
3. Cary impaling a chevron between three pears Orchard. Sir Philip Cary married Christian, daughter of William Orchard of Somerset.
4. Pawlett impaling a coat that shows ? a demi-lion in chief.
5. A much defaced shield charged with two chevronels impaling a pale wavy.
6. Pawlett impaling a fees and two mullets in chief.
7. Dinham impaling Arches. Sir John Dinham married Joan, daughter of Sir Richard Arches. Margaret, their fourth daughter married Nicholas Carew of Ottery Mohun, and their daughter Jane, married Cary.
8. Carew impaling Dinham.

Surrounding the rim, originally, were eight inscribed commemorative brasses of which only four remain: what message the lost brasses held is open to conjecture. Transcribed they read:

ROBERT CARY ESQUIRE, GAVE THE FONT ON THE SECOND DAY OF MARCH IN THE YEAR OF OUR LORD ONE THOUSAND ...

Fig 3. Commemorative brasses on Robert Cary's font, Cockington Church (PR).

A reputedly Elizabethan or Stuart octagonal font-cover, decorated with Renaissance-style carving, with two doors that opened for baptisms, was suffering damage due to the inquisitive poking of numerous fingers. Therefore for many years the cover stood out of harms way in the tower gallery, which precluded seeing it clearly; nowadays a window cill in St George's Chapel provides a more fitting home.

According to both Cresswell and Worth the cover's domed top, made by Harry Hems an eminent sculptor from Exeter, is a copy of the font-cover at Bramford, Suffolk, being added during the 1882-3 restoration. Worthy's *Devonshire Parishes in the Archdeaconry of Totnes, vol 2* depicts a photograph of a topless carved wooden font-cover attributed as Cockington's - curiously it is different to the cover now in the church.

Plate 15. Robert Cary's font and its wooden cover, Cockington Church pre 1932 (VC).

The pillars

The two rows of pillars dividing the nave from the north and south aisles are noteworthy; those in the north have plain capitals, whilst the southern have finely carved scroll and foliate decoration, each different. In addition, the half-capital at the southern aisle's western end has a carved mask of the Green Man. Mask-and-foliate carvings on capitals characteristically are Romanesque, c.1090-1100; however, in this instance, if we accept Watkin's date of c.1400 for the building of the south aisle, this example is perhaps much later.

The pulpit

Evidently the unusual but delightful wooden pulpit came to Cockington in 1825 redundant from St Saviour's Church, Torre, and used as a turkey house in a barn behind Cockington Court. Precisely when it moved to Cockington Church is uncertain. The attribution of the base is reputedly 15th century, whilst the upper part is possibly 16th-17th century. None of the rudely carved figures, which are similar to cherubs, are thought to be Christian - possibly they are symbolic with the sea. Two suggestions for the pulpit's origin arise - it perhaps formed part of the captured Spanish Armada vessel *Nostra Senora Del Rosario*, or, that it came from St Saviour's old rood screen? The latter can be discounted if the figures are not Christian.

Plate 16. Mask of the Green Man on the half-capital in the south aisle, Cockington Church 1989 (PR).

Plate 17. The pulpit, Cockington Church 1989 (BR).

The rood screen

A magnificent oaken rood screen with an intricately carved frieze depicting a vine complete with 16 birds perched in its foliage, each bird representing a different mood of the human soul, separates the nave and the chancel. Surmounting the central door, beneath the frieze, is a boss depicting the crowned Madonna holding the infant Jesus. Attribution of the screen is partially 14th century, but between 1916-20 Herbert Read of St Sidwell's Art Works, Exeter, completed extensive restoration.

Plate 18. The rood, Cockington Church, ? date (VC).

Plate 19. The Madonna-and-child boss on the rood screen, Cockington Church 1989 (BR).

The sanctuary
The Cary family vault

Beneath the sanctuary floor in front of the High Altar lies the Cary family vault. The rebuilding of the High Altar in 1933 obscured the vault. Interred within are Sir George Cary and two of his daughters (which two is uncertain, for he had three, Jane, Anne and one who's name is unrecorded). Sir George left instructions in his will that:

'In convenyent tyme he should be buryed in the Chapell of Cockington in a vault there, wherein two of my children do lye interred. And my further will and my desire is that my funerall should be solemnized in a decent and comely manner, and that on the day of my said funerall there should be given unto yea poore people of Cockington, and several parishes next adjoining, '£100', and after my said funerall and obsequies fynished my will and desire is that my said executors should in the said Chapell in my memory of me erect a decent and comely monument.'

Whether this monument materialised is unrecorded, but c.1883-4 Robert Sulyard Cary of Torre Abbey placed a memorial brass over the vault just inside the altar rails. Nowadays this brass is on the base step, but hidden by the carpet:

BENEATH THIS PAVEMENT LIE THE BODIES OF GEORGE CARY OF COCKINGTON, KNIGHT, LORD OF THIS MANOR AND SOMETIME DEPUTY OF IRELAND, WHO DIED ON 19th FEBRUARY 1617, AND DIVERS MEMBERS OF THE CARY FAMILY, IN PIOUS MEMORY OF WHOM THIS BRASS IS PLACED BY THE DESCENDANT, ROBERT S. CARY ESQ OF TORRE ABBEY.

On Saturday 5 August 1933, after the rebuilding of the High Altar, the Lord Bishop of Exeter, Lord William Cecil, held a rededication service. A memorial inscription reads:

THE ALTAR WAS PLACED IN THIS CHURCH TO
THE GLORY OF GOD AND IN MEMORY OF
JOHN FRY ROCKHEY OF THIS PARISH
WHO DIED 20 SEPTEMBER 1930 AND
JANETTA HIS WIFE WHO DIED 24 OCT. 1931

The reredos and altar rails

The reredos, a beautiful oil painting by J T Fouracre, depicts the Last Supper. Precisely when the unveiling and dedication ceremony occurred is uncertain, for one record states 28 August 1882 - a date refuted by the aforementioned Mary Janet's letter of 1881. The Jacobean altar-rails underwent restoration in 1901.

The priest's doorway, leper's squint, and piscina

In the north wall of the sanctuary, to the left of the High Altar, are the leper's squint and a walled-up priest's doorway, and on the right, in the south wall, a piscina stands c.45cm above the floor. The low height of the priest's doorway and the piscina's closeness to the floor indicates very clearly an anomaly in the sanctuary floor, undoubtedly caused by the rebuilding of the High Altar.

The misericords

Carved in the 15th century, two splendid wooden misericords adorn the north wall of the sanctuary. Reputedly they came from St Saviour's Church in 1825 - Cresswell said that at the time of the 1882-3 restoration of Cockington Church, one of them formed part of the clerk's desk. One depicts St Matthew standing between two angels, and the other shows St Luke standing writing his gospel between two ? winged-bulls. Above the figures on each misericord is a carved canopy, both of which show traces of an illegible inscription. This wall displays an even more ancient wooden misericord with a much abraded carved bust, evidently brought from Torre Abbey.

Plate 20. The leper's squint, Cockington Church 1989 (BR).

Plate 21. The walled-up priest's doorway with ancient misericord above,
two misericords, and the altar rails, Cockington Church 1989 (BR).

Plate 22. Enlargement of the ancient misericord on the north wall of the sanctuary, Cockington Church 1989 (BR).

Fig 4. Misericord carvings, Cockington Church (VC).

Plate 23. The piscina in the south wall of the sanctuary, Cockington Church 1989 (BR).

Plate 24. The Romanesque arch over the north aisle door, Cockington Church 1989 (PR).

The north aisle

The fine Romanesque arch above the doorway at the west end of the north aisle is one of two in the church.

Incumbents of Cockington

A list of incumbents of Cockington Church is displayed on the west wall of the north aisle:

THIS CHURCH
FORMERLY HELD BY TORRE ABBEY
WAS SERVED BY VICARS OF TORRE
UNTIL 1881

Thomas Sole Rundle	1882-1895.
James Henning	1895-1916.
Thomas Collins Walters	1913-1916.
Hubert Charles Studdy	1916-1936.
Marcus Knight	1936-1940.
Clement George Daw	1940-1947.
Frederick Roy Chatfield	1947-1972.
Prebendary of Exeter Cathedral	
John Colvin Donaldson	1973-1987.
Anthony K. E. Macey	1988-.

Memorials to Major C H Mallock and men lost in World Wars I & II

On the cill of the third window from the west rests Major C H Mallock's memorial cross; until autumn 1989 it graced St George's Chapel. Its wooden base-board bears the inscription GREATER LOVE HATH NO MAN THAN HE THAT LAY DOWN HIS LIFE FOR HIS FRIENDS. Flanking the left of Major Mallock's cross is a memorial board to the men of Cockington who died in the Great War, and on the right is another board to those who made the supreme sacrifice during World War II. Until 1989 the former board hung under the tower, whilst Rev Anthony Macey erected the latter in the same year. On the north wall hang several memorial inscriptions:

IN LOVING MEMORY
OF
CHARLES HERBERT MALLOCK D.S.O.
MAJOR ROYAL FIELD ARTILLERY
OF COCKINGTON COURT
SON OF
RICHARD AND MARY MALLOCK
BORN 15th MAY 1878
WHO GAVE HIS LIFE FOR HIS
COUNTRY 5 NOVEMBER 1917
AND RESTS NEAR YPRES AT
PROVEN

IN LOVING MEMORY OF
JOHN RAWLYN CHARLES MALLOCK
LT. COL: HAMPSHIRE REGIMENT
KILLED IN ACTION AT MALTOT 13 JULY 1944
SECOND SON OF MAJOR C. H. MALLOCK

IN LOVING MEMORY OF
ELIZABETH EMILY MALLOCK
WIFE OF RICHARD MALLOCK
AT REST 21 NOVEMBER 1927.

IN MEMORY OF
RICHARD MALLOCK
LORD OF THE MANOR OF
COCKINGTON AND CHELSTON
A MAN GREATLY BELOVED.
SOMETIME LIEUTENANT IN THE ROYAL
ARTILLERY, JUSTICE OF THE PEACE,
DEPUTY LIEUTENANT OF THE COUNTY
OF DEVON, COUNTY COUNCILLOR,
CHURCHWARDEN OF THIS PARISH OF
COCKINGTON, AND MEMBER OF
PARLIAMENT FOR THE TORQUAY
DIVISION FROM 1886 TO 1895.
BORN DECEMBER 28 1843.
AT REST JUNE 29 1900.

"THROUGH ALL THIS TRACT OF YEARS WEARING
THE WHITE FLOWER OF A BLAMELESS LIFE".
THIS TABLET PLACED HERE AS PART OF A
PUBLIC TRIBUTE TO HIS WORK.

THE NORTH SIDE OF THIS SCREEN WAS RESTORED IN
MEMORY
OF RICHARD MALLOCK, AT REST 29 JUNE 1900.

St George's Chapel

Concealed by a drape hanging on the north wall of St George's Chapel is the Romanesque arch of the north porch doorway. In 1941, for £146.6s, Herbert Read restored the chapel altar, dedicated to St George, which the Lord Bishop of Exeter, Dr C E Curzon, re-dedicated. This chapel, sometimes known as the Mallock Chapel, in most churches would be the Lady Chapel. Over the rood screen is the walled-up rood-loft doorway. The north wall has two memorial inscriptions:

IN MEMORY OF
WILLIAM THOMAS
FRANCIS
1866-1940
THIS ANCIENT CHAPEL WAS RESTORED
BY HIS LOVING WIFE
A.D. 1941

SACRED
TO THE MEMORY OF
CHARLES HERBERT MALLOCK
d.1823, AGED 70
AND OF MARIA HIS WIFE
d.1893, AGED 80
AND OF THEIR CHILDREN
MARY LOUISA
d.1857, AGED 20
AND
CHARLES HERBERT
d.1875, AGED 34

Plate 25. Memorial cross to Major Mallock DSO, Cockington Church 1989 (BR).

Plate 26. The Romanesque arch over the north porch doorway, Cockington Church 1988 (BR).

Plate 27. The walled-up rood loft doorway, Cockington Church 1989 (PR).

The funerary helmet

A heavy-cavalryman's iron helmet, reputedly Sir George Cary's, hangs on the north wall of St George's Chapel; prior to December 1936 it adorned the sanctuary. Confirmation came from the Keeper of Armour at the Royal Armouries H M Tower of London that this helmet formed part of a funerary achievement that formerly comprised spurs, gauntlets, shield and sword. As a funerary helmet, originally it would have had a painted grey ground; traces of painted gold decoration remain on the visor. The removal of a metal spike - holding a carved and painted wooden funerary crest - probably occurred in Victorian times; a crude repair with lead has filled the resulting hole in the combe.

In 1923 Cripps-Day, in Laking's *A Record of European Armour and Arms vol 5*, suggested that the Cockington helmet is made-up from pieces of various dates; however, an archaeological drawing, again commissioned especially for this book, disproved this hypothesis. The artistry revealed that it is entirely homogeneous and a good-quality Italianate or Low Country piece (perhaps Augsburg) dated c.1590, the characteristic signs being the style of visor ventilation holes and fastening-catch. If this helmet did belong to Sir George Cary, undoubtedly it was his everyday battle-helmet and not one acquired specifically for funerary purposes.

On the south wall is a memorial inscription:

ALTAR CURTAINS
GIVEN IN LOVING MEMORY
OF
FLORENCE GERTRUDE HOOPER
DIED DEC. 22nd 1987

Plate 28. The funerary helmet, Cockington Church 1989 (PR).

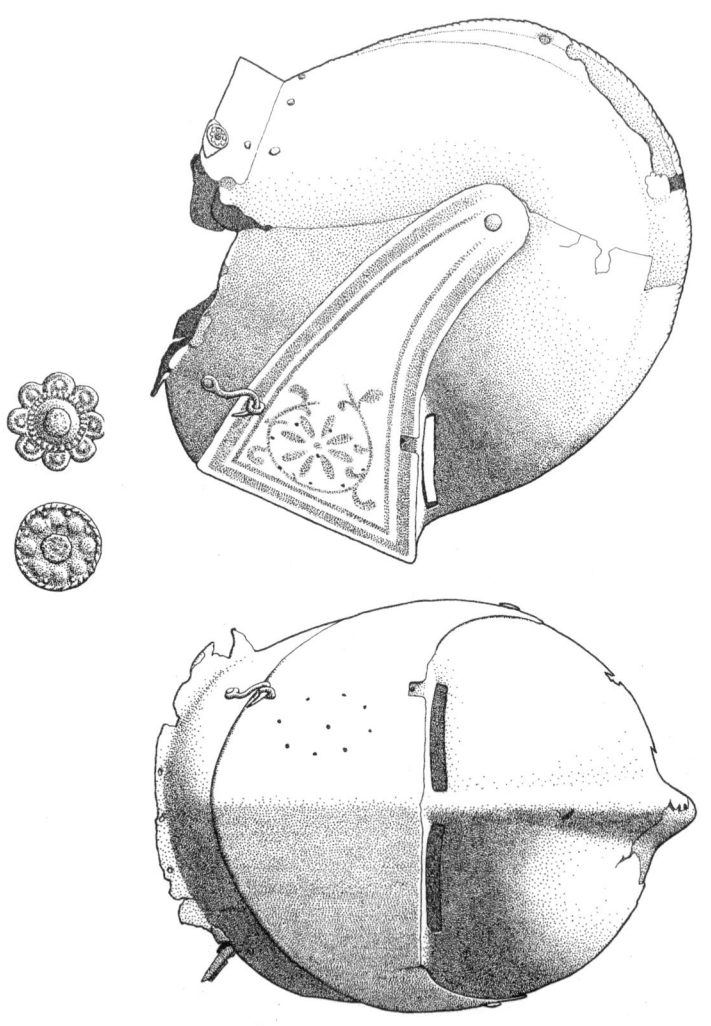

Fig 5. The funerary helmet, Cockington Church
(note enlargment of two styles of rivet-head decoration) (PR).

The parish chest

Cresswell observed in the 1920's that 'An ancient church chest, a "dug-out" of chestnut wood, with three locks' lay in the north chapel 'together with many fragments of carving'. Perceivably this chest was the original parish-chest. What became of the chest and the carvings is uncertain.

The south aisle
St Catherine's Chapel

At the eastern end of the south aisle, nowadays filled by the organ - made by Hele of Plymouth and given to the church by John Taylor on Easter Day 1892 (prior to this date stringed-instruments in the gallery provided the music) - lies St Catherine's Chapel; built into its rear wall is a 15th-century piscina. It was here that the Mallock family had their pew, which reputedly almost eclipsed the High Altar, and a fireplace to warm them in winter. A similar pew stood nearby for use by family servants. Affixed to the north side of the organ are two memorial inscriptions:

THIS
ELECTRIC BLOWER
WAS INSTALLED
TO THE
GLORY OF GOD,
IN MEMORY OF
LEONARD
HAWKES BRIERLY
WHO DIED
OCT 12th 1935

AT THE RESTORATION
OF THIS ORGAN BY
MR JOHN COULSON
IN 1970
THE COST OF THE ROHRFLUTE 9ft STOP
AND OTHER ADDITIONS
WAS DEFRAYED BY HIS WIDOW
RUTH
IN LOVING MEMORY OF THE LATE
CAPTAIN ARCHIBOLD GEORGE MORGAN, M. N.

G. ELLIOTT (ORGANIST & CHOIRMASTER)
ROY CHATFIELD (VICAR)

R. W. STICKLING
CHURCHWARDENS
E. C. WOOD

A further four memorial inscriptions hang on the south wall tucked away at the side of the organ:

TO THE GLORY OF GOD
AND IN LOVING MEMORY OF
JOHN TAYLOR
OF KILMORIE TORQUAY
WHO DIED NOVEMBER 9th 1903
ALSO OF
JULIA ELIZABETH
HIS WIFE
WHO DIED NOVEMBER 27th 1905

THIS ORGAN WAS COMPLETED IN
OCTOBER 1901 AS A MEMORIAL OF
JOHN TAYLOR
LIETENANT IN THE
1st KING'S ROYAL RIFLES
ELDEST SON OF JOHN AND JULIA G. TAYLOR
OF KILMORIE, TORQUAY AND FORMERLY
OF CHELSTON TOWER IN THIS PARISH.
HE SERVED WITH HIS REGIMENT IN INDIA,
MAURITIUS AND SOUTH AFRICA
AND FELL IN ACTION AT TALANA HILL,
NATAL, ON OCTOBER 20th 1899.
AGED 26

AUGUSTUS HENRY DELL HUTTON M. A.
PRIEST OF THE CHURCH OF ENGLAND.
ENTERED INTO REST JANUARY 20th 1899.
THIS MEMORIAL OF HIM IS PLACED IN
THE CHURCH OF S. GEORGE AND S. MARY,
COCKINGTON,
WHERE HE LOVED TO SERVE AS A VOLUNTARY
HELPER, BY HIS FRIENDS WHO REVERENCE HIS MEMORY,
J. HENNING, VICAR

THE SOUTH SIDE OF THIS SCREEN WAS RESTORED IN
MEMORY OF JAMES
HENNING, PRIEST, VICAR OF THIS PARISH, 1895-1913 AT REST
11 JUNE 1913

Affixed to the left-hand side of the vestry door is a memorial inscription:

IN MEMORY OF
WILLIAM DAVY
PARISH CLERK WHO
SERVED THIS CHURCH AND
PARISH OF COCKINGTON
FOR NEARLY FIFTY YEARS
HE ENTERED INTO REST
DECEMBER 31st 1899

——— .. ———

THIS MEMORIAL OF HIM
IS PLACED HERE BY PARISHIONERS
AND FRIENDS WHO GREATLY
ESTEEMED HIM
"THE LORD GRANT UNTO HIM THAT HE
MAY FIND MERRY OF THE LORD IN THAT DAY"

The vestry

Before 1720 the vestry was a porch with a priest's parvise situated above it; this chamber, although somewhat enlarged, is extant. An inscribed commemorative stone in the north wall of the vestry indicates that the porch underwent rebuilding in 1720; until 1938 this stone was over the external doorway of the porch. Although no constructional evidence is apparent, allegedly, communicating doors from the parvise and the north part of the tower allowed the priest to cross the gallery. A 14th-century stone window-surround built into the parvise's eastern wall came from the south wall during the 1720 transition.

The sanctuary knocker and parvise squint

The door between the south aisle and the vestry has a hinged-peephole and a medieval iron sanctuary-knocker. The latter was removed from the outside of the door and placed in its present position at the time of the

1720 alteration - its mark is clearly visible on the vestry side of the door. Abolition of sanctuary rights at Cockington occurred in 1623. Above the vestry door is the parvise squint reopened in 1914.

Fig 6. Parvise inscription, Cockington Church (PR).

Plate 29. 14th-century window-surround in the parvise, Cockington Church 1989 (BR).

Plate 30. The vestry door, Cockington Church 1989
(note sanctuary knocker and hinged-peephole) (PR).

Plate 31. Opposite side of vestry door, Cockington Church 1989 (note mark of original position of sanctuary knocker, and hinged-peephole) (PR).

Plate 32. The parvise squint, Cockington Church 1989 (PR).

Memorial inscriptions on the church floor
The nave

HERE LIETH BURIED JANE THE WIFE OF JOHN
EASTLEY OF STAUNTOR ...... DEVON GENT.
WHO DIED YE 12 DAY OF MARCH 1698 AND WAS A
SWEET AND DEAR MOTHER OF SEVEN CHILDREN
CETAT SUCE 72

HERE LIETH BURIED MARY THE DAUGHTER OF JOHN
EASTLEY WHO DIED THE FOUTH DAY OF JUNE ANNO
DOM 1699

HERE LYETH BURIED JOHN EASTLEY OF STANTOR
GENTLEMEN WHO DIED THE 1 DAY OF APRIL ANNO
DOM 1720 (NATUS 14 FEBY 1648) AETATIS SUAE
HERE ALSO ARE
DEPOSITED THE REMAINS OF YARDLEY EASTLEY OF
PAIGNTON
GENT WHO DIED NOVEMBER THE 25 1789

HERE LIETH BURIED JOHN TAYLOR OF COCKINGTON WHO
DIED THE 7th DAY OF APRILL ANNO DOM 1717 HE MARRIED
JANE THE DAUGHTER OF JOHN EASTLEY OF STAUNTOR GENT.
SACRED TO THE MEMORY OF MR JACOB LEY WHO DIED
3 SEPT 1788 AGED 63 YEARS ALSO OF ELIZABETH HIS WIFE
WHO DIED 1 APRIL 1831 AGED 91

The north aisle

HERE LIETH THE BODY OF SUSANNA THE WIFE OF
JOHN BARBOUR WHO DEPARTED THIS LIFE DEC'R THE 7th
1712 AGED 64 RELATED TO RAWLIN MALLOCK ESQ
MEMENTO MORI

HERE LYETH THE BODY OF ANN BARBOR YE DAUGHTER
OF JOHN AND SUSANNA HIS WIFE OF THIS PARISH WHO
DIED YE FIRST DAY OF OCT'R ANNO D 1702 AGED 19
YEARS.
READER AS THOU PASSES BY
STAY AND LEARN THY DESTINY
IN Y SPRING AND FLOWERING MAY
DEATH HATH CROPT MY LIFE AWAY
AND HERE I LAY IN HOPE TO RAISE
AMONG THE SAINTS MY GOD TO PRAISE
I DOE BUT WAIT UNTILL THE DAY
MY LORD SHALL CALL - COME ANN AWAY
ONE HILLS AND DALES LET CYPRUS GROW
WHILE PHILOMEL MOURNS HERE BELOW
THIS VIRGINS TO HER LOWLY HEARSE
COME TO HER SHRINE AND LEARN A PIOUS VERSE
DELICIA JACES NECNON ET CURA PARENTUM
GAUDIA D. B - INE HEA MEA FATA. VALE
SO HERE I LY MY PARENTS JOY AND CARE
BE MY SAD FATE THEIR JOY'S NOW ENDED ARE.
WHO DE
HERE LIETH THE BODY OF MR JOHN BARBOR OF
COCKINGTON
PARTED THIS LIFE 15 MAY A.D. 1717

(Carpets obscure other memorial inscriptions on the church floor.)

Dispute over right of way

After many centuries of alleged unrestricted passage to Cockington Church, in 1929 a disagreement arose between Richard Mallock and the church authority as to precisely who had the right to pass along the Churchway through the park. Richard had grown tired of inquisitive visitors peering through the windows of Cockington Court, and cars obstructing the

Churchway. After lengthy and fruitless discussion between the two parties the church authority initiated legal proceedings against Richard Mallock. Between 27 November and 4 December 1931 the case was heard in the High Court of Justice, Chancery Division, who found '… that there was no record of there ever being an express dedication of public right of way', therefore the action failed and was dismissed, with costs awarded to the defendant.

Burials

Unlike most parish churches Cockington does not have its own graveyard. Lang commented:

'But in the 1929 enquiry into the church path right of way, his lordship enquired whether there was a burial ground attached to the church. He was told that the position was rather mysterious, as there were registers of burials extending over many years and several people, including persons of distinction, were buried in the church. There was some evidence that part of the garden of Cockington Court might have been a burial ground, as some gravestones and possibly bones had been found there.'

This mention of 'gravestones' and 'bones' seems to have some foundation, for Lang appears to be relating a story written by Ellis in 1931. He stated that a visitor to Cockington Court, Rev A J Baker of South Newton (near Salisbury, Wiltshire), had a "Commonplace Book" in which, under the date 21 July 1901, it is recorded that a gardener called Richards dug up in Cockington Court garden, fragments of a wooden coffin, black with age, containing a leg and thigh bone.

In addition, Ellis observed:

'There are no less than 1,298 burials recorded in the Register between 1632 and 1882. These interments are not to be found in Torre Churchyard; therefore there must have been a churchyard at Cockington which is now lost.'

Interestingly, the *Overseers' of the Poor Accounts* (hereafter OPA) hold four entries for burials, although the place of interment for these lamentable unfortunates is unrecorded:

'1752   Paid the Minister for Burying of Rich'd Snelling 00.03.00.
1754   Paid for a Box to bury Humphrys Child in   00.01.00.
1757   Paid for Bering of Joan Smardon the pagon   00.03.00.
1778   Paid for making yea grave of Bridgett Rendell   00.01.06.'

The *Burial Register* informs us of one *Nicholas* Snelling's burial on 6 October 1752 - not *Richard* Snelling. Perhaps either the overseer of the poor or Tormohun's vicar made a mistake when scribing the name? However, possibly it is not an error, therefore the *Burial Register* does not record Richard's interment. Curiously, the three other burials are not entered therein either? Whether these folk were Cockingtonians or visitors is uncertain, nonetheless the *Burial Register* should hold their names. Therefore we have to account for the burial place of some 1,302 souls - if not at St Saviour's, logically, perhaps all are indeed in a Cockington Church forgotten graveyard?

The most likely place for a graveyard would be the area of the old tennis-courts, and feasibly their construction uncovered evidence of burials. Did Richard Mallock suppress gardener Richards discovery and also withhold it from the 1931 right of way court action? Interestingly, the *1801 CEM* shows a distinct enclosure to the west of the church, with a gap in its eastern boundary; this is the same area as the old tennis courts and it may well have been a graveyard.

In early times, normally only parish churches had a graveyard, although in some circumstances, such as prevailed at Cockington, other churches received permission. This writer tends to agree with Ellis that the Parish of Cockington did have its own graveyard and that it was situated at the above location. If this is true, it is very apparent that the terraces formed by the tennis-courts required the excavation of such a great depth of soil that many of its graves were removed and dumped elsewhere. Nonetheless, perhaps sufficient evidence remains in situ. This enigma will only be solved by archaeological survey or chance discovery during any future ground disturbance.

Lang said the final resting-place of some Cockingtonians was Marldon, in the graveyard of the Parish Church of St John the Baptist. However, Marldon's *Burial Register*, which dates between 1598-1881, is devoid of entries for Cockington parishioners (so far as clarity allows), and inspection of the gravestones produces a similar negative result; therefore it must remain unconfirmed.

There is a tale that many years ago park gardener Charlie Fey dug up human bones - possibly the remains of plague victims - in the dell (since backfilled with spoil excavated at Hollicombe Gas Works) on the right-hand side of the path leading to the bridge and down to the ponds. For Charlie this led to a three-day spell in hospital where, allegedly, his town hall superiors told him to *forget* what he saw. His widow, Violet, confirmed that indeed he did uncover some bones and other material, which he reported to his employer, but she did not recall if it led to his hospitalisation.

It would be foolish to dismiss this tale as being a deliberate fabrication of the truth, for although we have no record of how the Black Death's several visitations affected the parish, it would be unlikely for there not to be at least one mass burial-place of pestilence victims somewhere within its borders. Daddy Croft on Kingsland Hill springs to mind (see vol 1)? Of course, there is the possibility that these remains represent some other luckless individual, for in times past it was not uncommon to bury corpses at places other than churchyards. Another point worth considering - is this the place where Richard Mallock dumped soil (and its contents) dug out from the tennis-courts?

Cockington Vicarage

On 7 July 1882 Miss Champernowne laid the foundation stone for Cockington Vicarage at the top of nowadays Vicarage Hill on a site given to the church by Richard Mallock. Completed in 1883, the church authorities sold this imposing traditional sandstone residence in June 1987 and replaced it with a new-built vicarage in Monterey Close, Livermead.

Plate 33. The old Cockington Vicarage, Vicarage Hill, Chelston 1989 (PR)

Chapter Two

Cockington Court

Cockington Court, a Department of the Environment listed Grade II Georgian mansion retaining elements of its former Tudor and Stuart splendour, stands in the north-west of Cockington Park. Originally, so certain writers have noted, before the addition of the two wings, the medieval house formed a square around a quadrangle entered between two towers. Whether this is the correct understanding is impossible to prove, for primary archival material is absent (so far as is known). The ground immediately at the rear of the current house is some three metres higher than the ground floor, which means that the original house, as described above, would not have extended in that direction. For such a plan building, on this selfsame site, it would have been considerably smaller. Whatever, it is here, sometime between 1070-80, that William de Falesia probably erected the first stone-built Cockington manor house.

A more picturesque setting for a lordly residence would be hard to find, facing sweeping Front Lawn and protected at the rear and sides by gently rising ground, encompassed by majestic trees. Cited in 1654 we find 'Foremeade', ME 'front', 'front', and OE 'mâêd', 'meadow' - 'land in front of a great house', and in 1676 'Great Meadow', both of which are perhaps what is now known as Front Lawn.

Cary influence

In 1588 the Carys added a gable-roofed and mullion-windowed wing to the south-west side of the medieval house; the right-hand corner of its cornice has the carved date 1577, and the left-hand corner depicts the very abraded initials TC. The implication of these chiselled inscriptions is

70

uncertain; perhaps George Cary meant them as a memorial to his father Thomas? The sharpness of the numerals suggest they are not original.

Fig 7. Cockington Court, redrawn from Archdeacon Froude's sketch of 1679 (PR).

Plate 34. Cockington Court c.1913 (TNHS).

Plate 35. Cast-iron horse-tethering post, Cockington Court stables 1989 (PR).

Plate 36. Driver Jim Short in his Hackney Carriage, Cockington Square c.1970's (JS).

Mallock alterations

Rawlyn Mallock I rebuilt the north-east wing in c.1673; he utilised a style similar to the wing in the south-east, thereby disguising the lofty medieval kitchen. Similarly carved in this wing's cornice are the initials RM on the left-hand corner and 1673 on the right-hand (which also allude they are not contemporary), undoubtedly a memorial to its builder. About 70 years after Spain's Armada of 1588 Rawlyn I demolished the old forecourt perimeter walls and a gate-house on the south-west side, and replaced them with lower walls and pillars on which hung iron gates. He transformed the medieval central hall into three stories, the minstrels' gallery became several rooms, and a parapet-surmounted hipped gable-roof replaced the pitched roof. A new front-doorway appeared, with three windows on each side at ground floor level, seven windows on the first floor and the second floor, five.

A re-drawing by Rev James Henning (Vicar of Cockington) of a 1679 sketch of the Court and Cockington Church by Archdeacon Froude shows a small building (perhaps a cottage) at the foot of the slope leading to the church. This sketch also depicts what appear to be more buildings on the north-west side of the Court. All of these structures probably disappeared during Rawlyn I's so-called 'improvements'.

Next to leave his mark on the Court was Rev Roger Mallock; by 1800 he had removed the top-storey of the central block, including the converted minstrels' gallery, and removed the gable of each wing. Additionally he demolished a range of 'antique offices' (perhaps the buildings shown on the 1679 sketch?) and Rawlyn I's forecourt wall and gateway. However, apart from destruction, the stables and poundhouse at the rear of the north-east wing are probably his creations, for the *1801 CEM* depicts them. For many years the stables, which retain some original fixtures and fittings, housed park gardeners, as well as a tack-room for Hackney Carriage horses. Currently, various craft industries use this outlying part of the Court, and other outbuildings provide a tack-room.

Before 1945, the year when Herbert Reeves brought the first landau carriage to Cockington, gigs ran a passenger service back and forth along Cockington Lane between Cockington Square and Torbay Road at

Livermead seafront. Nowadays, during the tourist season, a number of landau carriages ply the same route; an additional service between Cockington Court and Cockington Square commenced in 1994. A Hackney Carriage licensing system operated as early as 1894, and Torquay Borough Council continued with licences in the days of the gigs. In addition, each gig driver required a separate licence; this system remains in operation today. Outbuildings at the rear of Cockington Court provide storage for some of the carriages when they are idle.

The porchway pillars

The front-porchway's much-weathered stone pillars, each of which comprises three drum columns, are an enigma. The fluting on the lower drum columns, particularly the left-hand pillar (facing the door), does not match the middle and upper, which indicates that each pillar comprises two, or even three, separate pieces, of which none are compatible. Each middle drum column is 20cm long and has on its rear, facing the wall, a very abraded or defaced carved possible coat of arms. The emblem on the left-hand pillar appears to be a square enclosing a circle and cross; the right-hand emblem is similar, but more difficult to interpret.

The age of the pillars and the attribution of these possible arms, and when or why they perhaps suffered obliteration, is uncertain. Some say that the arms are those of the Carys, cut out and reversed after Roger Mallock purchased Cockington in 1654. Ellis, however, suggested that Rev Roger Mallock erected the pillars 'In an attempt to create a more dignified appearance' which if true, negates such a hypothesis. The 1679 sketch of Cockington Court depicts what appears to be two pillars at the front-porch which if the same as the present ones would disprove Ellis' story. Their weatherbeaten appearance creates the impression of some considerable age, certainly anteceding the late 18th century. If Rev Roger Mallock did erect them, possibly they were already made-up and came from elsewhere. To have carved emblems means they were, at one time, of some importance. Did they originate at Cockington Court or from some other building? A local theory suggests that they came from Berry Pomeroy Castle.

Plate 37. Front porchway pillars, Cockington Court 1992 (PR).

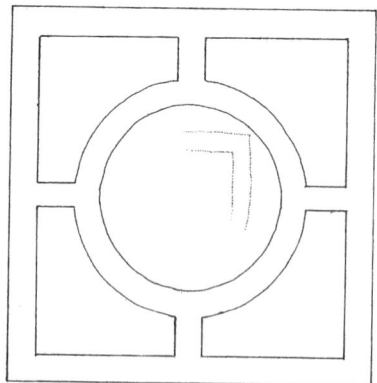

Fig 8. Front porchway pillar emblem, Cockington Court 1989 (PR).

Some external and internal features

E llis observed:

'At the time of W H Mallock all that remained of note in the house were several Italian ceilings, a panelled dining-room of the William and Mary period, a number of portraits dating from James I onwards, and a wallpaper depicting natives standing and dancing under palm trees, apparently plundered during the Napoleonic Wars from a captured French vessel.'

However, apart from the aforementioned William and Mary panelling and an ornate plaster ceiling in the former dining-room, panelling of the same period is found in a first floor room of the north-east wing. This room also boasts a fine stone-built fireplace attributed to the Elizabethan or Stuart era; beneath the main stairway on the ground floor is a similar fireplace. Walnut panelling in the former library reputedly is from the trees that once graced Higher Chelston's Walnut Road, and the wooden dog-leg staircase in the north-east wing is undoubtedly partially Elizabethan. There is no basis for believing the often quoted "three courses of medieval bricks visible at the bottom of the central block, between the two wings" - bricks are not evident here.

Acquired by Richard Mallock c.1883 at Barnstaple, adorning the former drawing-room is a splendid oaken chimney-piece carved with intricate stylised foliate, hominoid masks, serpents and griffins. Sections are 17th-century English, with perhaps some Flemish work, whilst most of the remainder is 19th-century English reproduction. The exceptions are a marquetry square panel, which replaces an inlaid coat of arms, and a pair of marquetry asymmetrical panels; all probably came from a 16th-century Germanic Nonesuch chest.

At the foot of the main staircase, illuminating and overlooking the entrance hall, is a striking stained-glass window illustrating the four seasons. Additionally it has 46 individual panes each depicting the letter 'M'. These letters perhaps signify Mallock or Richard Mallock's wife

Mary? The external stonework beneath the window reveals a much older stone-cill the implication of which is that the window-opening has at some time been made smaller. Alternatively, perhaps it is a walled-up doorway that formerly led to the outside?

Outwardly the only other visible evidence of the Court's Tudor and Stuart past is a trio of stone-mullion windows, one of which is walled-up, and a stone-built doorway-surround in the north-east wing. Two more small window-openings of this period, both walled-up, one below and to the right-hand side of the stained-glass window at the rear, and the other, which retains some glass, is at first floor level on the north-east side. These walled-up windows probably represent a desire to lessen the burden of William III's Window Tax, first levied in 1696 to finance his great re-coinage of the same year.

Plate 38. Former dining-room, Cockington Court 1988 (note William and Mary panelling, and Italian ceiling) (PR).

Plate 39. North-east wing first floor room, Cockington Court 1988 (note Elizabethan/Stuart fireplace and William and Mary panelling) (PR).

Plate 40. Former library, Cockington Court 1991 (note walnut panelling) (PR).

Plate 41. North-east wing partial Elizabethan staircase, Cockington Court 1988 (PR).

Plate 42. The oaken chimney-piece in the former drawing-room,
Cockington Court 1989 (note marquetry panels) (BR).

Plate 43. Stained-glass window, Cockington Court 1988 (BR).

Plate 44. Stone cill, possible walled-up doorway, and Tudor/Stuart
walled-up window, rear of Cockington Court 1988 (PR).

Plate 45. Tudor/Stuart stone-mullion windows (one walled-up) and stone-built doorway surround, north-east wing of Cockington Court 1988 (PR).

Plate 46. First floor Tudor/Stuart window, rear of Cockington Court 1988 (PR).

Other occupants and uses

A t the conclusion of the Great War a Yorkshire coal mine owner, Major J H Charlesworth, leased Cockington Court for seven years. Since acquisition by the local authority, parts of the Court have fulfilled a variety of uses, for example, a café, ice cream factory, staff flats, and beach-department equipment store. For years suggestions were proffered for a more fitting employment, they include: time-share flats, horticultural training centre, and golf-course club-house, none of which Torbay Borough Council (hereafter TBC) approved, and meanwhile dereliction gained a foothold.

A working party of TBC parks committee in 1970 investigated the Court's future, who reported part might be suitable for staging an exhibition of Peter Clapham's collection of West Country costumes, dating between 1760-1930. Apart from period-costumes a suggestion arose for displaying pottery, pewter and farm vehicles. In order to do this it would be necessary to execute repairs and alterations, which would cost c.£20,000, and another possibility was to invite private tenants. The committee decided that whatever the use, they should avoid commercialisation and any extension of the usage of the Churchway or car park - the house must stay in existence and also not stand empty. As before, this idea fell short of TBC's requirement and faded away.

In 1988 TBC started refurbishing Cockington Court; this entailed stripping much of the ugly internal alterations. Devon Rural Skills Trust (hereafter DRST) took over the house in early summer 1989; they aimed to promote traditional rural crafts, thereby transforming it into a 'living' building once again. Sadly, this union proved short lived, for in October 1993 DRST left Cockington.

After the demise of DRST, TBC promoted various crafts-people within the Court and in the old stables and poundhouse area at the rear. From 1 December 1999 Torbay Coast And Countryside Trust, a newly founded charity, whose function is to 'protect and enhance the best of Torbay's green open spaces', became the official occupiers of Cockington Court. The aforementioned crafts-people continue to manufacture and sell their products.

In 1991 Lord Falkland, a descendant of the Cockington Carys, unveiled a Torbay Civic Society plaque near the main entrance:

TORBAY CIVIC SOCIETY, COCKINGTON COURT, MANOR HOUSE OF THE SQUIRE OF COCKINGTON FROM SAXON TIMES TO 1932.

Notable events at Cockington Court
Royal visitors

Torbay, on occasions, has proved a popular haunt with members of both the British and overseas royalty. On 23 October 1868 Queen Sophia of Holland paid Torquay a 13-day visit and on 28 February 1870 returned for 11 days; on one of these trips she decided to take a look at Cockington and whilst there called at the Court. A daughter of Richard Mallock, who happened to be the only member of the family at home, received a summons to present herself to the queen, who wished to inspect the house and its surrounds. The royal personage also availed herself of a visit to the church, escorted by the young Miss Mallock.

After suffering the illness diphtheria in the winter of 1886, the Princess of Wales spent some time convalescing in Torquay's mild climate and on 9 and 26 March graced Cockington Court with her presence. In commemoration of the latter visitation the Duchess of Sutherland, who resided in Torquay, planted an oak sapling - grown from an acorn sown at the time of Major C H Mallock's birth - on the front lawn (whereabouts is uncertain). On 23 October 1896 Princess Louise and the Marquis of Lorne arrived in Torquay for a week's stay and paid a visit to the Court.

Agatha Christie

Agatha Christie, the Torquay-born novelist, was a great friend of the Mallocks, and as a young woman she spent many happy hours at the Court participating in amateur dramatics with the family.

Lord Rothermore

In order to avoid the London Blitz during World War II, Mr Coscinsky evacuated to Cockington Court press baron Lord Rothermore's £250,000 art collection. As Lord Rothermore's advisor he had become concerned for the collection's safety and suggested a safer refuge would be prudent and recommended Torquay. At the time Lord Rothermore was in Bermuda and when he received Mr Coscinsky's recommendation he cabled back asking whether Torquay was safe; in turn he received a reply, saying: 'Only Heaven safe - but no accommodation!'

Out of gratitude for being allowed to keep the collection at the Court Mr Coscinsky arranged a special exhibition of some of the finest pieces, held from Easter until 31 October 1941. The opulent display filled several rooms to which members of the public gained admission, where they viewed many of the treasures. One of the finest was a *Book of Hours* with a golden clasp and bindings made by Benvenuto Cellini. Pope Clement X gave this book to the wife of Francis I who in turn presented it to Katherine of Aragon. Considered to be the next finest piece was a unique figure of the Eighth Chinese Immortal carved from a single block of flawless amber more than 40cm high. Sadly, Lord Rothermore expired before having the opportunity to view his collection in their temporary home.

Hauntings at Cockington Court

When he was about 15 years old, in the late 1940's, Tony Perryman lived with his parents in one of the staff flats in the south-west wing of Cockington Court. One winter's evening, whilst alone in the house with his dog who was sleeping by the lounge fire, the animal suddenly woke and stood, with hair erect and tale horizontal, and stared at the closed door. Tony, who thought his parents had returned home early, opened the door and went with the dog into the short length of passage leading to the transverse gallery that runs the length of the building. Not normally a timid beast, the dog refused to enter this main passageway and it was some considerable time before it regained its composure and ventured beyond the immediate limits of the flat.

The above tale perhaps has a connection with other occurrences experienced by one Mr Gliddons, head gardener in Cockington Park in the late 1950's and early 1960's, who lived in the same flat - occasionally he had seen a ghostly nun in one of the bedrooms. This selfsame apparition, allegedly, regularly manifested itself to one of the last Mallock daughters to reside in the house - it would sit on her bed and hold conversations with the young girl. Allegedly, a sad-looking cavalier roams the Court - perhaps tragic Sir Henry Cary bemoaning the loss of his ancestral home?

Chapter Three

Hostelries

The Church Inn or Church House

Richard Mallock gave a talk on 21 January 1895 at the Chelston Coffee Tavern, where he said:

'In 1531 there appears to have been two inns in the parish of Cockington; the landlord of one was named William Cornelys and the second was John Wal.'

We find recorded under the date 1641'... ¹/₂ of dwelling house in Cockington called the Church house ...' By 1654 one 'Thomas Ball' held 'Moity [¹/₂] of the Churchhouse' and in 1708-9 'William Ball a sailor' was the landlord. This inn is traceable again in 1735 and 1740. Lang commented:

'An old village pub stood on the site of the present Drum Inn. Named the Church Inn, it was pulled down in 1831, but according to William Winget,writing in 1914, the ruins still remained.'

However, this statement is inaccurate, for on 14 February 1914 Winget actually observed:

'Opposite the almshouses formerly stood the Church Inn, the ruins of which still remain; and close by is the lane and path leading to Stantor and Marldon.'

There is no documentary evidence of an earlier inn on the site of the *Drum Inn* (although the *1801 CEM* does show a building here). Winget's lane undoubtedly is the trackway nowadays known as Bewhay Lane. A disbursement in the OPA seems to corroborate Winget's *Church Inn* '1725 Pd the Church House for Beer 00.02.00'. It is probable that the *Church Inn* and *Church house* were one and the same.

New legislation enacted in 1553 limited the number of taverns (a house allowed to sell wine in addition to beer and ale). For example, Exeter, the most populous town in Devon, had an allowance of only four. At this time, therefore, Cockington village was unlikely to have had more than one tavern, although there may have been an alehouse (premises for brewing and selling beer and ale) and/or an inn (a place that also provided food and accommodation). Whether prior to 1553 Cockington village, or the parish, had other such establishments is uncertain.

The Anzacs pub

Don Mills related an interesting story concerning a public house situated in Cockington Village, at the Bewhay Lane Cockington Lane junction, within living memory:

'One day in 1980 Henry Veale, an ex-Torquinian who now lived in Australia, came into the Weaver's Cottage and reminisced on old Cockington. As a boy, during the Great War, Henry had a delivery round in Cockington and Chelston. One of his regular calls was to an old lean-to single-storey wooden pub with a rear wall made of thick cob at the bottom of Bewhay Lane. At one end a door led into the bar, on the right-hand side of which were two large wooden casks - one held ale and the other cider. Rude wooden tables and bench seats were the only furniture. At the far end of the bar was a door that opened into a small room used by the landlord. Built into the rear cob wall was a fireplace and a small niche that held a draw for the takings. The main customers were farmworkers, but during the war Anzacs, who had a camp in the watermeadows in lower Cockington valley, patronised the pub.

Towards the end of the war a fire completely destroyed the wooden part of the building.'

We can be fairly certain that this simple structure was of no great age, for it is absent from the *1906 Ordnance Survey* (hereafter OS) *Map*. If it did disappear before the end of the Great War and if we can accept the accuracy of the OS, it could not have been older than 12 years; probably it leant against a far older cob wall that previously had formed part of another building.

Again the *1801 CEM* helps solve this mystery, for it shows a building on Bewhay Lane's northern corner with Cockington Lane, whilst in 1846 two buildings stood here; their platforms, an old gateway in Cockington Lane, and rear access lane remain beneath the undergrowth. Moreover, the *1801 CEM* depicts four buildings fronting Cockington Lane on the southern side of its junction with Bewhay Lane, evident by their extant terraced platforms, a garden wall, gateway and path. Therefore any of these latter buildings, or perhaps one of the two buildings (possibly the smallest) formerly behind the site of the *Drum Inn* (see vol 3), or indeed the one beneath it, could have been one of the village's other drinking-establishments of yesteryear.

A relative of the Mallocks, Arthur Mudge of Plympton, wrote in his diary further evidence for what may have been one of the former such establishments:

'6 February, 1879
In the afternoon, Dick, Edward & self proceeded to take down the old house by the almshouses - We fixed two charges of powder viz 4lbs & 2lbs in one corner & affected a breach, we then converted a fir pole prop into a battering ram & knocked down a good bit of the wall, but the roof did not fall in - Friday was wet in the morning & I carpented but it cleared up so we again attacked the house till 2pm when Richard had to go & attend a meeting. We wasted a good deal of time trying to get the ram into position; finally we affected another breach in the wall with 5lbs of powder.

10 February, 1879
Another wet day but still we are determined to have a good turn at the old house, so down there we went and with the help of ram & powder got down one side - a terrible mess are we all in.
12 February, 1879
Had another turn at the old house, very successful. Freeman came & we got down [with] powder & ram a very large piece of it.
18 April, 1879
Dick, Jack, Edward & myself again attacked the old house, using powder with great success & blew down the remainder of it with the exception of the big chimney which we have left for a future date'.

Regrettably, Arthur did not explain precisely where this 'old house' stood in relation to the almshouses (built c.1806, see vol 4). As the only visual evidence of razed buildings in the immediate vicinity are the aforementioned in Cockington Lane, on the northern and southern corners of Bewhay Lane, it implies, therefore, that one of them would have been Arthur's 'old house'. Unless some secreted, dusty archive has further evidence of this old building's final fate we shall never know if the remaining section of wall succumbed to Arthur's and Richard's bombardment. Perhaps it did not and that the 'big chimney', which would have formed an integral part of a substantial wall, was the 'thick cob wall' forming the rear wall of Henry Veale's lean-to pub. This old cob wall is the only corroboration of a visible above ground ruin on the site of any of these former buildings - presumably this was the remains of Winget's old *Church Inn*.

The Drum Inn
Today the Parish of Cockington has only two public houses, the *Haywain* on the corner of Sherwell Valley Road and Queensway, and the *Drum Inn* in Russel Park Lane, Cockington Village.
The famous architect Sir Edwin Lutyens RA designed the imposing thatch-roofed *Drum Inn*, which occupies part of the site of a former sawmill, as the centre-piece for Cockington Trust's (hereafter CT) proposed new village. Originally destined to be the Forge Inn (and to be

somewhat larger with a fine garden also designed by Lutyens) CT amended the name as it might be 'Prejudicial to the celebrated forge in the village'.

Covering 522 sq.m the *Drum Inn* cost c.£7,000 to build, using 16th-century-style bricks especially made in Belgium to Sir Edwin's own specification. London's Cenotaph, another of his creations, provided the model for the chimneys. Apparently the main contractor was Sherwell Builders, in reality Cockington's Behar family. Many traders contributed towards the inn's completion, including: G Hingston & Son, master thatcher of Broadhempston; Higgins & Cattle Ltd of London, light fittings; G N Haden & Son of Torquay, plumbing; John Bolding & Sons Ltd of London, sanitary fittings; Gaskell & Chambers Ltd of London, beer engines, cellar and bar fittings; J F Rockhey Ltd of Torquay, curtains and drapery; Samuel Snawden of Yealmpton and Williams & Cox of Torquay, furnishings; Allams of Torquay, china and glass; and E H Sermon of Torquay, cutlery and electro-plate.

All fixtures, fittings and furnishings complied with Sir Edwin's specifications. Glassware, tableware, cutlery and linen depicted a crest comprising a drum and crossed drumsticks, whilst menus, cards and letterheads had a trademark of a little drummer boy. This drummer boy appears to be the same as Dame Laura Knight's design for the clock inn-sign (discussed later).

More of Sir Edwin's creations - four carved wooden figurine lamps painted black and gold - reputedly remain hidden above the false ceiling in the old buttery. One - either a lion passant or a rampant unicorn - is mounted in each corner of the room. Identical carvings formerly graced what used to be the public bar - these disappeared during one of the many alterations.

A lounge bar window once held a pane engraved with a poem named 'The Drum' presented to Sir Edwin Lutyens by its composer, Laurence Whistler. When Bill Allan took over as manager in 1958 he found the engraving discarded and gathering dust in the cellar and replaced it in the original window-frame. Sometime between the end of October 1961 when Bill left and Bert Taylor's arrival in January 1974 someone removed it yet again. Bert discovered it in a cupboard and had it framed and placed on display inside the pub; nowadays it hangs on a wall in Drake's Bar.

For many years the *Drum Inn* was a true inn, the upstairs rooms being used for accommodating guests. From its opening on 23 May 1936, when owned by CT, until 25 October 1946, when the Prudential Assurance Company Ltd (hereafter Prudential) purchased much of Cockington Village, it was a freehouse. On 25 December 1946 Ind Coope (Oxford & West) Ltd, trading as Hall's Brewery (formerly Ansells Brewery), acquired the lease and this company (nowadays Ansells Retail Ltd) has held it ever since (at the time of writing, a merger with another company is pending).

Initially it proved somewhat difficult to obtain a licence in respect of the proposed *Forge Inn*. When Sir William Phene Neal, chairman of CT, first applied to Torquay Magistrates Court on 5 March 1934, the court heard many arguments, both for and against, some by men of national reputation. Despite the evidence of witnesses for the applicant the Bench refused on the grounds that 'A sufficiently strong case had not been made'. A number of Cockingtonians and off-licensed hotels of Torquay objected because the contemplated inn would not be a residential hotel but merely one selling wine and spirits. This they feared would interfere with the livelihood of Torquay's other wine and spirit merchants; they also felt the presence of a public house would 'alter the character of the neighbourhood'. When the *Drum Inn* first started trading, it sold food and alcohol-free drinks only, the landlord eventually obtained a liquor licence, but for the sale of beer only , from Mondays to Saturdays, remaining closed on Sundays.

On a lighter note, at a later application for a spirit licence, which the court had refused on more than one occasion, one of the witnesses on behalf of the applicant, Sir William Phene Neal, was Scottish weaver John Mills, resident of Cockington's Weaver's Cottage (see vol 4). John informed the Bench; 'Folk a' knockin' at m' door at all 'oors of the night wantin' t' know where they could get a wee dram.' His evidence influenced the Bench to approve the spirit licence; when addressing the court the magistrate commented, 'It seems, Mr Mills, we should be granting you the licence!'

The sheet-copper inn-sign is noteworthy: the *Torquay Times* of 5 June 1936 cited:

'The sign to be displayed outside will be a drummer boy. In reality this is a clock, which will signify the passing of each quarter of an hour by a roll on the drum. At one time a special painting was done for the inn by Dame Laura Knight, and it was from this that the clock-maker made his figure.'

The *Herald Express* of 22 May 1946 reported:

'The name Drum Inn was inspired by a painting executed by Dame Laura Knight, R. A., of a drummer boy in the 18th century uniform of the Devon Regiment. The painting will be a model for a clock which will form the sign for the inn. The model drummer boy will roll his drum each quarter of an hour and chime the hours.'

Waycotts Sale Catalogue of Cockington Village 1946 depicts a picture of 'The Drummer Boy' the caption of which reads 'Designed by Dame Laura Knight, R. A., and is the trademark of the house'.

General consensus is that the clock inn-sign never materialised and there is no record of what became of Dame Laura's painting of a drummer boy. Interestingly, some people say they can remember a sign depicting a drum and drumsticks only. A photograph of the South Devon Hunt, taken c.1945, shows the same inn-sign as the one now hanging here - a man garbed in Elizabethan costume beating a drum. Originally, the sign hung on an oaken post standing in the flower bed uphill of the main entrance door; however, sometime between August 1984 and 1986 the post became unsafe, therefore a replacement was re-sited at the bottom of the entrance driveway.

The *Drum Inn* lease is the only authentic record confirming that Dame Laura Knight was indeed the artist responsible for painting the Drum Inn sign:

'At all times during the said term to maintain and display in its present position or other position approved by the Landlords and use their best endeavours to preserve the existing copper inn sign of the Drum Inn (painted by Dame Laura Knight D.B.E.I.R.A.).'

Plate 47. The Drum Inn, Cockington Village c.1936 (TM).

Plate 48. Sketch of the Drum Inn, Cockington Village 1936 (IS).

Fig 9. Drum Inn utensils crest (PR).

Fig 10. Little Drummer Boy, trademark of the Drum Inn (W & PR).

Plate 49. Dame Laura Knight's Drum Inn sign 1987 (BR).

Plate 50. Cockington Estate staff and tenants Christmas and farewell party at the Drum Inn 1946 (DM).

Key to identification (where known).
1 Mrs Kerslake, **2** Thomas Kerslake, **3** Maurice Behar, **4** Mrs Behar, **5** Miss Ward, **7** Mrs White, **15** ? Mrs Vinnicombe, **16** Harry Vinnicombe, **23** ? Mrs Fey, **30** Mrs Pook, **31** Miss Denbow, **32** John Mills, **33** Mrs Tranter, **36** ? Mrs Rook, **37** Jack Rook, **39** Mr Johnstone, **46** Margaret Mills, **47** Mr Tranter, **49** Tom White, **50** Frank Palk, **51** George Denbow, **60** Jack (John) Denbow.

The Drum.

Drake left a drum to Englishmen,
And bade them beat & wake him when
Perils upon his England come
But now where can we find that drum?

You who stand & closely peer,
Curious to read what's written here,
And see the light of English skies
Silver the glass, & bless your eyes,
Think of the England old & green
You wander & are happy in,
And if the hour of perils come
Find, in your own loud heart, that drum.

Fig 11. Laurence Whistler's poem 'The Drum' (BT).

Legend of the Drum

Whilst supping a pint in the *Drum Inn* one may overhear locals discussing the origin of the pub's name, which they say has an association with two feuding local families, in distant times, that had gone on for many years without being resolved and has nothing to do with Drake's Drum. Eventually, one family, who lived on one side of Cockington valley, decided to try and end the dispute, so they sent a drummer boy on a peace mission to the other family who lived on the opposite side of the valley. They rejected this offer, cut the lad's throat and stuffed his body inside the drum and rolled it back down the hill - where it came to rest is the spot where the Drum Inn now stands.

However, there is another version of this tale and it is one that possibly has more substance. It concerns the Carys and another local family, of slightly lower standing, who had disputed the ownership of a particular meadow for a very long time. In an attempt to settle the argument the less prominent family decided to send a deputation of six retainers and a drummer-boy to Cockington Court proffering an olive branch. This incensed the Carys, who considered it an insult, and they promptly killed the boy and returned his body with the retainers back to whence they came. The distraught lesser family passed a curse on the Carys, which was that the first male-born child of future generations would not succeed the family title. The Cary pedigree reveals that some males who were first in line to the title did indeed die before doing so, and the earliest occasion this happened is the death of Robert Cary's first son (prior to 1540).

Although the preceding two tales are undoubtedly pure fantasy imparted as mischievous banter, feasibly they stemmed from a dispute (and one associated with Drake's Drum) between two prominent local families that actually did occur in the 16th century. In 1588 the Privy Council instructed Cockington's George Cary and Compton's Sir John Gilbert to allow 4d per day in respect of the guarding and welfare of each Armada Spaniard captured from the *Nostra del Senora Rosario*. Sir John Gilbert did not take kindly to this order and refused to pay his share, therefore George Cary had to pay double. Due to this, it appears relations between the once good friends became rather strained and remained that way for a long time.

By 1592 the Spanish were again threatening England and it was necessary to prepare against this danger. The Privy Council appointed six Devonshire gentlemen, including George Cary and Sir John Gilbert, to each raise a regiment from their estates. On 6 September 1592 the Privy Council sent a letter to George Cary enquiring why he had failed to organise his regiment, to which he replied on 28 September 1592 'that it was due to Sir John Gilbert claiming jurisdiction over some of his lands whose tenants he was enrolling and thus enforcing himself to go for his band 20 or 30 miles away'.

As a result, the Privy Council, on 12 August 1593, ordered all men in the hundred of Heytor to enrol under George Cary. Sir John's reaction was to complain, saying that he had mustered 1,000 men in Torbay when the Spaniards were about and that Cary had lain quiet. History tells us that later George Cary received a knighthood and ascended to a higher station, whilst Sir John Gilbert remained somewhat out of favour with Elizabeth I. There is no record whether the two men ever resolved their difference, but clearly this may well have been the source of the legend of the *Drum Inn.*

Cider-making

From at least 1437 Cristina Cary made cider at Cockington Court, but the whereabouts of her poundhouse is unknown. Parish records hold many mentions of cider, for example in 1437 two pipes of cider being sold for 12/8d. One John Bourton in 1654 held 'poundhouse', whilst 'Pound Parks' and 'Pound' are cited under the dates 1654 and 1723, respectively. However, the latter two perhaps have an association with a livestock pound, OE 'pund' - 'enclosure for stray animals'. In 1654, before he inherited the estate from his father Roger, Rawlyn Mallock I leased to Christopher Martyne of Chelston the 'Poundhouse', and in 1768 we find 'Pound House Meadow, alias the Scrowl by Ford Meadow' which implies it was alias Forda Meadow near present-day Goshen Road at Lower Chelston (see vol 3). By 1820 'Cider Pound' occurred, and in 1839 Stantor had a 'Cyder pound'. Whether John Bourton and Christopher Martyne leased the same poundhouse, or if it was indeed the Court's 1437 poundhouse, remains unknown. No doubt customers of the lost drinking-establishments of the parish consumed much of Cockington Court's cider.

As late as the mid 1940's the Denbow brothers milk-cart pony, Sally, powered the poundhouse supposedly built by Rev Roger Mallock at the back of Cockington Court's north-east wing. Village boys, including Tom Mills from Cockington's famous family of weavers, and Laurence Fey, harvested cider apples from local orchards - a task for which, allegedly, they received little pay. After work the boys would often sneak back into the poundhouse and surreptitiously siphon a small quantity of cider for their own refreshment - this they classed as 'postage due'. A sorry pile of parts removed from the old cider-press, until recent times lay heaped in the yard at the back of the Court.

Bibliography

Books

Cox, J C. Churchwardens' Accounts from the 14th century to the Close of the 17th century. 1913.

Cresswell, B. Notes on Devon Churches in the Deanery of Ipplepen. 1921.

Criticus. The Churches and Chapels of Torquay. 1905.

Davidson, J. Church Notes of South Devon. M S. c.1840.

Ellis, A C. A Historical Survey of Torquay. 1930.

Ellis, A C. Royal Occasions in Torbay. 1935.

Laking, J F. A Record of European Armour and Arms, vol 5. 1923.

Lang, J F. Old Cockington, vol 1. 1971.

Peskett, H. Guide to the Parish and Non-Parochial Registers of Devon and Cornwall 1538-1837, extra series vol 2. 1979.

Pike, J R. Torquay, Torbay: A Bibliographical Guide. 1973.

Polwhele, R. Parochial History of Devonshire. 1793/1806.

Read, B A. History Beneath Our Feet. 1988 & 1995.

Read, B A. Cockington Bygones, vol 1 1999, vol 3 & 4 forthcoming.

Richardson, J. The Local Historian's Encyclopaedia. 1974 & 1986.

Risdon, T. Survey of the County of Devon. 1811.

Seymour, D. Torre Abbey. 1977.

Stabb, J. Some Old Devon Churches, vol 1. 1908-16.

Vivian, J L. Visitations of the County of Devon 1531, 1564, and 1620. 1895.

White, J T. The History of Torquay. 1878.

White, W. History, Gazetteer and Directory of the County of Devon. 1878-9.

Worth, R N. History of Devonshire. 1886.

Worthy, C. Devonshire Parishes in the Archdeaconry of Totnes, vol 2. 1889.

Miscellaneous

Churchwardens' Accounts for Cockington 48/13 - 8/8/124, 9/1-2, 9/5, PW1 V & PW3 B.

Department of the Environment. List of Buildings of Special Archaeological or Historical Interest. 1975.

Donaldson, J C. Rev. The Parish Church of St George and St Mary.

Dymond, R. The Manor of Cockington. 1882.

Ellis, A C. Cockington and its Church. 1936.

Ellis, A C. Working Notes.

Lang, J F. Working Notes.

Mudge, A. Diary of. 1878-80.

Overseers' of the Poor Accounts for Cockington. 48/13 -9/3.4 1665-1836, 9/6 1768,9/71852-3, 9/8 1750-2, 9/9 1854, 9/10 1860-1.

Parish Register of Cockington. MF1-3, 6.
Parish Register for Marldon. MF1-2 & MF2-4.
Packe, J. A Walk of Historical Interest and Natural Beauty Through the Village of Cockington.
Parish Archives in St Matthew's Church.
Rowe, M. Calendar of Mallock Documents. 1959.
The Cockington Trust Ltd. Cockington, its History and its Future. 1933.
The Drum Inn Lease.
Torquay Natural History Society. Place-names of Cockington, vol 4. 1922-6.
Walker, H. Cockington. 1985.
Watkin, H R. Working Notes.
Watkin, H R. Cockington Parish Church. 1914.
Waycotts Cockington Sale Catalogue. 1946.

Maps
A Plan of the Parish of Cockington with part of the Parish of Marldon. 1801. PWDRO. 81/X36.
Ordnance Survey Map 6-inch and 25-inch. 1906.

Index

gas works 68
Gaskell & Chambers Ltd 91
gate-house 73
gauntlets 53
Georgian 70
Germanic 76
gigs 73
Gilbert, Sir John 100-101
Gilham
    Arthur Frederick 13
    Mrs 13
glass
    painted 29-31
    stained 30, 76, 81
Gliddons, Mr 86
God 30, 56-57
Goad, Thomas 60
golf course 83
graffiti 23
grave
    stones 66, 68
    yard 66-68
Great Meadow 70
griffins 76
gunpowder 89-90

Hackney Carriage 72-74
Haden & Son, G N 91
Hall's Brewery 92
Hampshire Regiment 48
hauntings 85
Head, Hilda Mabel 16
Hearder, Mr 22
Hele of Plymouth 56
Hems, Harry 32
Herald Express IX, 93
heraldic 23
heraldry 31
Heytor, hundred of 101
Higgins & Cattle Ltd 91
High Court of Justice 66
Hingston, G, & Son 91
Hollicombe 68
Hooper, Florence Gertrude 54
Horsely, Vince 4

horse tethering-post 72
horses 73
hospital 68
hostelry, pub, alehouse, tavern, inn 6, 87-88
    Anzacs pub 88
    Church house, or House 87-88
    Church Inn 87-88, 90
    Drum Inn 7, 87-97, 100-101
    Forge Inn 90, 92
    Haywain 90
Hours, Book of 85
Humphrys child 67
Hutton, Augustus Henry Dell 58
Hydon, Edward 22

ice cream 83
incumbents 47
Ind Coope 92
India 58
initials 70, 73
inn sign 91, 93-94, 97
Ipplepen, Deanery of 10
Ireland 39
Italian 76-77
Italianate 54

Jacobean 40
Janet, Mary 15, 40
Jesus V, 37
Johnstone, Mr 98
Justice of the Peace 49

Kan, George 21
Keeper of Armour 53
Kerslake
    Mr 98
    Thomas 98
Kingsland Hill 68
Kilmorie 57-58
Knight, Dame Laura 91, 93-94, 97
Ladypark V
Lady Chapel 49
Laking, G F 53
landau carriage 73-74
Lang, Joan 4, 66, 68, 87